Move It!

Motion, forces and you

Written by **Adrienne Mason**
Illustrated by **Claudia Dávila**

Kids Can Press

Kids Can Press gratefully acknowledges the financial support of the Government of Ontario, through the Ontario Media Development Corporation; the Ontario Arts Council; the Canada Council for the Arts; and the Government of Canada, through the CBF, for our publishing activity.

Published in Canada and the U.S. by Kids Can Press Ltd.
25 Dockside Drive, Toronto, ON M5A 0B5

Kids Can Press is a Corus Entertainment Inc. company

www.kidscanpress.com

The artwork in this book was rendered in Photoshop.
The text is set in Century Gothic.

Edited by Valerie Wyatt
Designed by Julia Naimska
Science consultant: Jean Bullard

Printed and bound in Tseung Kwan O, NT Hong Kong, China, in 11/2017 by Paramount Printing Co. Ltd.

CM 05 0 9 8 7 6 5 4 3 2
CM PA 05 20 19 18 17 16 15 14 13 12

Library and Archives Canada Cataloguing in Publication

Mason, Adrienne
    Move it! : motion, forces and you / written by Adrienne Mason ; illustrated by Claudia Dávila.

(Primary physical science)
Includes index.
ISBN 978-1-55337-758-0 (bound)   ISBN 978-1-55337-759-7 (pbk.)

1. Motion — Juvenile literature. 2. Force and energy — Juvenile literature.
I. Dávila, Claudia II. Title. III. Series.

QC133.5.M383 2005   j531'.11   C2004-905153-9

Contents

Push and pull

You use pushes and pulls to make things move. A push moves an object away. A pull brings it closer. A push or a pull is called a force.

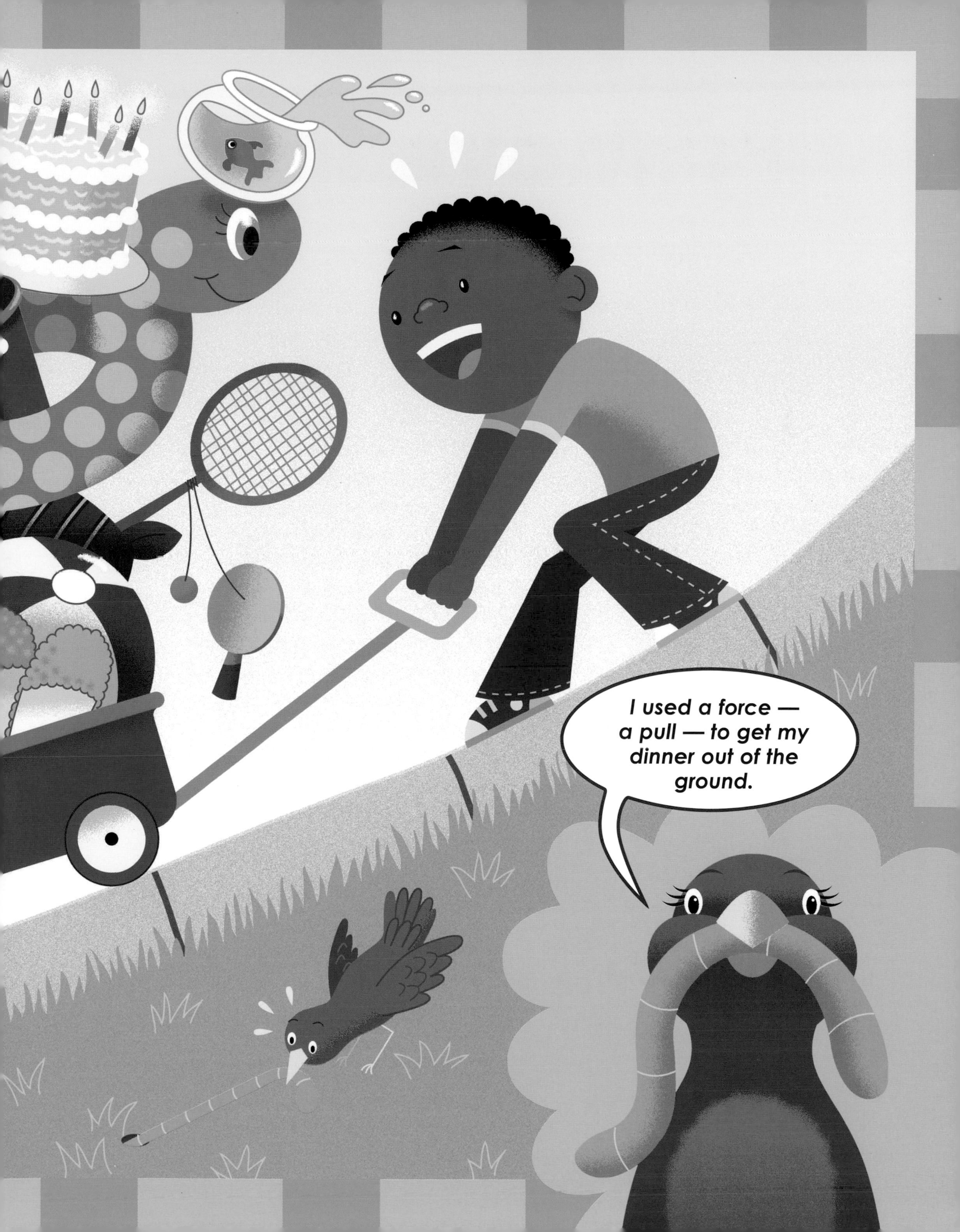
I used a force — a pull — to get my dinner out of the ground.

Move it!

You use force to move your body. To walk, you push against the ground. You also use force to move things. You pull a wagon to make it move.

Can you find five ways these children are using force to move their bodies or other things?

Push it!

It takes force to move things. Does it take more force to move heavy things? Try this to find out.

You will need
- 3 identical, opaque plastic tubs with lids
- small rocks or marbles
- uncooked macaroni or other small pasta
- crumpled paper

What to do

1 Fill one tub with rocks or marbles, one with pasta and one with crumpled paper.

2 Put the lids on the tubs. Ask a helper to move the tubs around until you don't know which is which.

3 Push each tub across the table. Which tub took the most force (the biggest push) to move? What do you think is in it? Which took the least force (the smallest push) to move? What do you think is in it? Remove the lids to see if you were right.

What's happening?

It takes more force (a bigger push) to move heavy things, like the rocks. It takes less force (a smaller push) to move lighter things.

Make it move

Things do not move unless they are pushed or pulled. When you lift something, you are pulling it up. When you throw something, you are pushing it away.

Can you find five ways these children are using pushes or pulls to make things move?

Go the distance

To throw a ball to someone far away, you need to use a lot of force (a big push). To throw to someone closer, you need less force. The more force you use to move something, the greater the distance it will move.

Puffing power

Does a big force make things move faster?
Try this to find out.

You will need

- a Ping-Pong ball
- a drinking straw

What to do

1 Place the Ping-Pong ball on a table.

2 Move the ball by blowing through the straw at it.

3 Blow softly. What happens? Blow harder. Does the ball go faster or slower?

4 Have a race with a friend to see who can make their ball go fastest.

What's happening?

When you use a small force (blow lightly), the ball moves slowly. When you use a bigger force (blow harder), the ball moves faster.

The more force I use to push against the water, the faster I move.

Move it on over

When you kick a ball it moves in a straight line, unless it is then kicked from the side. All things move in a straight line unless they are pushed or pulled from a different direction. A kick is just a push with your foot.

I was flying in a straight line until a gust of wind blew me in another direction.

Stop it!

To stop something that is moving, you need to use force. You stop a ball by pushing in the opposite direction.

The faster something moves, the more force it takes to stop it.

Down to Earth

If you throw something up, it will fall back down. It is pulled down by a force called gravity.

You can't see gravity, but it pulls things — including you — down toward Earth. This is why things fall to the ground when you drop them.

Lift it!

It takes force to overcome gravity and lift things. Does it take more force to lift heavy things?

You will need

- a small nail
- a small, empty yogurt tub
- three 15 cm (6 in.) long pieces of string
- a rubber band
- marbles or small rocks
- a ruler

What to do

1 Have an adult use the nail to make three evenly spaced holes around the rim of the plastic tub.

2 Thread one piece of string through each hole and tie a knot to hold the end in place.

3 Tie the free ends of the string together. Slip the rubber band through the knotted end as shown.

4 Put the tub on the floor and add one marble. Hold the elastic band by the end and pull up until the plastic tub lifts off the floor. Measure the length of the elastic.

5 Add 5 marbles to the tub and repeat step 4. Does the length of the elastic change when there are more objects in the tub?

What's happening?

The force of gravity pulls down on the tub. You need to pull up against gravity to lift the tub. The marbles make the tub heavier, and it takes more force (a bigger pull) to lift it.

The more force you use to lift the tub, the longer the elastic band stretches.

Slow motion

You push on the pedals to make your bicycle move. When you stop pushing, your bicycle slows down and stops. Why?

Your bicycle tires are rubbing against the road. When two surfaces rub together there is a force called friction.

Friction makes moving things slow down and then stop. Friction also helps you grip the ground when you walk or run.

Without some friction between my feet and the ground, I would slip and slide all over the place.

Sliding along

Friction happens when things rub together. Is friction always the same? Try this to find out.

You will need

- a bread board
- an eraser
- a small stone
- a small wooden block
- an ice cube

What to do

1 Put the bread board on a table. Line up the eraser, stone, block and ice cube at one end of the board.

2 Carefully lift the end of the board until one object begins to slide. Lift more and watch how fast the objects slide. Do some slide faster than others? Why do you think this is?

3 Try other small objects you find around the house. Which one slides best?

What's happening?

There is more friction between some materials than others. With the rubber eraser the friction is greater. With the ice cube the friction is less.

There is not much friction between my smooth shell and the snow.

Get moving!

A force is a push or a pull that starts an object moving or changes its motion.

A force can start an object moving.

28

A force can stop a moving object.

A force can change the direction
of an object that is already moving.

For parents and teachers

The information and activities in this book are designed to teach children about forces and motion. Here are some ways you can explore the concepts further.

Push and pull, pages 4–5
Objects are moved by pushing or pulling. When you are out for a walk or on the playground, have children describe whether various actions are pushes or pulls. Explain that when they walk, run or jump, they are pushing against the ground.

Move it!, pages 6–7
There are many ways to describe moving things, such as pushing, pulling, lifting, twirling and jumping. Put on some music and make up a dance that consists of a variety of movements. Ask children to describe all of the movements they made. Which were pushing movements and which were pulling movements?

Push it!, pages 8–9
More force (a bigger push or pull) is required to move heavier things. Test other objects and ask children to predict how much force (a little or a lot; more or less) will be needed to move them.

Make it move, pages 10–11
Things move by transferring force from one object to another. For example, when a child pushes a toy car, she is transferring force from her muscles into a pushing force on the car.

Go the distance, pages 12–13
The strength of a force applied to an object affects how far it will travel. With more force, an object travels farther. Experiment with this idea by having children use different amounts of force to kick a ball or push a toy car. Measure or note how far the ball or car travels each time.

Puffing power, pages 14–15
The strength of a force applied to an object affects how fast it will travel. With more force, an object travels faster. In a large space, have children roll a ball over a set distance. First, roll gently and see how long it takes to travel the distance. Then apply more force and compare the results.

Move it on over, pages 16–17
Objects usually move in a straight line unless another force is applied. Objects will change direction if pushed or pulled from the side. During a soccer or hockey game, balls and pucks are always changing directions as other forces are applied. Explore this idea by having children kick a rolling ball.

Stop it!, pages 18–19
Objects stop moving in their original direction when they are pushed or pulled in the opposite direction. Children could play catch to explore this idea. Ask children if they have ever caught, or been hit by, a fast-moving ball or puck. If so, they

know it can hurt. The ball or puck is exerting force on the child's body. It takes more force to stop a fast-moving ball.

Down to Earth, pages 20–21
Gravity is a pulling force. Earth's gravity pulls things downwards. To explore gravity, ask children to predict what will happen when you toss a variety of objects into the air. Toss lighter or heavier objects, such as a running shoe, a crumpled paper and a coin.

Lift it!, pages 22–23
The heavier the object, the more force is needed to overcome gravity and lift it. The elastic band serves as a force meter in this activity. Have children compare lifting an empty pail and a pail full of stones or marbles. Which requires more force to lift?

Slow motion, pages 24–25
Friction is caused when one object rubs against another. Although friction slows things down, it is an important force. A certain amount of friction ensures that objects do not slide off surfaces. Have children examine different surfaces, such as those on running shoes, sleds, bicycle tires and baking sheets. Why do they think these objects have smooth or rough surfaces?

Sliding along, pages 26–27
The amount of friction varies depending on the materials that rub together. Try dragging an object over different surfaces, such as a carpet, a sidewalk or tiles. Tape or tie an elastic to the object and observe how much the elastic stretches as the object is dragged over the different surfaces. The elastic acts as a force meter and gauges the amount of friction — the more friction the longer the elastic stretches.

Get moving!, pages 28–29
This summary explains the main principles of forces and movement.

Words to know

force: a push or a pull

friction: a force that happens when two objects rub together

gravity: a force that pulls objects toward Earth

Index